Published by Dymaxicon
Sausalito, CA

ISBN 978-1-937965-16-7
www.dymaxicon.com

Ristretto Roasters logo by Bethany Ng
Portrait of Din Johnson on p. 6 © Justin Tunis
Photo on p. 16 © Steve Lovegrove
All other photography © Michael Harper

DYMAXICON

HOW TO MAKE
COFFEE

Before You've Had Coffee

Ristretto Roasters' spectacularly simple
guide to brewing at home

by Din Johnson

CONTENTS

Ristretto Roasters' Din Johnson at the Nicolai St. Cafe

INTRODUCTION

For some of us, the hardest task of the day is brewing a cup of coffee in the morning— it's a Catch-22: How do you wake up enough to make yourself some coffee before you've had that first cup of coffee?

This single-minded little book is about one thing and one thing only: teaching you easy, bulletproof methods for brewing a spectacularly good cup of coffee even when you are standing half-awake in your own kitchen.

Like any ritual, brewing coffee well requires that you do a few things right, in a certain order, every time. What coffee brewing does not require is that you drop a bunch of dough on fancy gear. Contrary to conventional wisdom, you do not need to go out and buy a multimeter, a thermocouple and a linear particle accelerator to make a cup of coffee every bit as good as the one poured by your favorite neighborhood barista. You probably won't spend any more on coffee than you are spending now.

COFFEE CHEMISTRY

Really craving that first cup of coffee in the morning? You're not alone. More than 2.25 billion cups of coffee are consumed daily, making coffee one of the top three commodities in the world, jockeying for position with water and oil.

Clearly, we love coffee. But what engenders that love, that daily need? Sure, it's the caffeine, a naturally occurring stimulant that is present in the bean. It's also because coffee is good for you: it's terrifically high in antioxidants, it boosts your metabolism, and every month there's a new study showing coffee's health benefits. Seriously, have some coffee. It tastes good, and is good for you.

We all feel marvelous after drinking a great cup of coffee, and that's because some pretty marvelous things are happening in the bean. Here are a few:

Wetting: You grind your coffee, you wet the grounds... look at that: it's puffing up! That's called a "bloom," and it occurs as the bean fibers absorb hot water and gas is driven from the coffee particles and the small spaces inside the grounds. This prepares the grounds for the extraction of soluble elements. Note that only freshly roasted coffee will bloom.

Extraction: During this second phase, the water-soluble flavoring compounds dissolve, rapidly moving out of the bean fibers and entering the water.

Hydrolysis: In this last stage, large molecules of water-soluble carbohydrates break down into smaller molecules that only then become water-soluble. These are mostly sugars, but also include some proteins.

★ COFFEE CHEMISTRY ★

Light

On the lighter end of the spectrum, beans can be the color of cinnamon. A light roast is usually chosen to highlight the acidity or piquancy characteristics found in coffee—think crisp white wine. A light roast usually yields a brew with a tea-like mouth feel.

Medium

Once you move into a medium roast, the sugars naturally present in the coffee start to caramelize, leading to a greater sense of weight on the tongue, i.e., body and sweetness. To continue the wine analogy, we are moving into red territory.

Dark

Dark roasted coffee is that black, oily bean that makes most serious coffee lovers cringe. Have you ever seen someone order a filet mignon well done, then watched them saw through the brick of meat every bit as appetizing as a charcoal briquette? Does the thought make you shudder? That's how coffee geeks feel when you order French roast (which isn't a type of coffee bean, but a roasting level).

Extra-Dark

No.... just, no.

ROAST LEVELS

That bin of ink-black glossy beams in your neighborhood market may seem powerfully alluring, maybe it's a French roast, and you are sure that the deep, rich, glossy sheen of oil on the surface must mean that a bold, rich, flavorful cup awaits.

Entirely a myth, so let's dispel it: those ebony beans have been over-roasted to a fare-thee-well, annihilating the delicate flavors they once possessed. All of that furious charring action has caused the bean itself to turn to carbon, and all of the beans' precious oils to leach to the surface, where, exposed to oxygen, they quickly begin to turn rancid. Those oils are where the flavor of the coffee reside. Your eye may see richness in the surface gloss, but that is only because the richness that makes for complex flavor and a robust mouth feel has been removed from the coffee bean itself.

The keepers of the great caffeine-industrial complex have led us to believe the carbonized flavors of over-roasted coffee are what connoisseurs mean when they use words like "robust" or "full-bodied." Not true! A truly robust and flavorful bean is about substance, not flash—it will appear matte and dry to the eye—as the oils are still held within the bean, to be released only upon grinding and brewing.

BUYING THE RIGHT BEANS

Coffee beans are like fruits, in that they have a window of optimum freshness. 3-7 days from the roast date is best.

The roast date should appear printed or hand written on the bag. If it doesn't, you probably aren't dealing with the kind of roaster who takes freshness seriously, or who doesn't roast in batches small enough to ensure quality. In the first couple of days after roasting, the coffee is still off-gassing. Optimal drinkability is between 3 and 4 days after the roast date. This is not to say that you cannot drink coffee that's older, but the coffee is at its prime in this window, able to showcase all its best characteristics.

Always buy whole bean coffee, not the pre-ground kind, however cleverly vacuum packed. As soon as coffee is ground, oxidation begins and flavors deteriorate quickly.

STORING COFFEE

Let's dispel another myth: coffee should never be stored in either the refrigerator or the freezer. Coffee is very sensitive to moisture and temperature, and any foods you have in your fridge or freezer will impart flavors to the coffee. Nobody wants frozen lima bean-flavored coffee!

Coffee's enemies also include air, heat and light. The best way to store coffee is in an airtight container in a cool, dry place. Even if you live in Miami, you have a dark cupboard (and hopefully air-conditioning). Keep your coffee there.

Fine

Like table salt.

Levels 1-3.

Medium

Like Kosher salt or cornmeal.

Levels 4-6.

Coarse

Like bread crumbs or couscous.

Levels 7-10.

THE RIGHT GRIND

Accompanying each set of brewing instructions you will find this graphic scale recommending the ideal grind level for that method. As a general rule, you can think of grinds as fine, medium and coarse, but many grinders have settings labeled 1-10.

Not sure if your device's 5 is a medium grind? We've given you some common household items for reference. Grab some Kosher salt and compare. And don't worry; it's not an exact science and is very much a matter of preference. Grind on a 5 and brew some coffee, then feel free to go up or down a notch to find the sweet spot for how you like your coffee.

Just remember: the finer you go on the grind, the faster the coffee will extract. For instance, French press calls for the coarsest grind because the coffee is submerged in water for the entire brewing process. If you used a fine grind here, your coffee would be sludgy, over-extracted and bitter.

THE RIGHT RATIOS

Coffee is a potent agent, the acceptable range of concentration being 8.25 grams of ground coffee to every 4 oz. of water. Officially, the Specialty Coffee Association of America recommends 9-11 grams of ground coffee per 6 ounces of water as a "minimum starting dose." Unofficially, it's your kitchen, and you should feel free to experiment with different doses and grind levels.

So what's in a gram? Buying a $10 kitchen scale that measures grams probably won't kill you, and it will make your morning coffee-making process that much more mindless (which is what we all want, no?). But if you prefer, you can use any handy measuring receptacle. Once you've figured out your perfect ratio, just measure out the same amount every time, and you'll be golden.

A lot of people tend to be timid about using too much coffee, when in actuality using too little coffee is the single most common mistake rookie home brewers make. As soon as you start skimping on the coffee you risk over-extraction, which results in a bitter, thin cup. So don't be afraid to dose that coffee a little higher! If you are going to experiment, try to err on the side of using more coffee rather than less, and see where that takes you.

THE THREE T'S:
TIME, TEMPERATURE, TURBULENCE

"Think of each particle as a tiny sponge: the smaller the sponge, the less water you need to saturate it," says Ristretto Roasters barista MaryCeleste Gorman. "The rate at which your coffee drips will also depend on its country of origin, and how it was processed." MaryCeleste's brewing tips, forthwith:

Time: If the brew is too long, you will end up with a bitter cup. Try making the grind coarser. If you brew too quickly, you will end up with a sour cup. Try a finer grind.

Temperature: This is the second-most important variable when making coffee. Water that is too hot will bring out more acidity in the cup. Water that is too cool will bring out sour notes in the cup.

Turbulence: This is what causes coffee particles to separate and thereby allow a uniform flow of water to pass through the coffee. The problem that occurs when there is not enough turbulence is a failure to coat all of the coffee bed, resulting in an uneven extraction. Too much turbulence will create an overly agitated brew, the coffee extracting too quickly, resulting in a cup that will be bitter.

WHAT'S A "CUP"?

You just purchased your dream coffee brewing system, and on the carafe is a fill line that reads "8 cups." But "cup" here does not refer to the 8-ounces a measuring cup holds. Here cup is just manufacturer lingo for something loosely defined as a serving of coffee, and exactly what that is supposed to mean can vary widely from one brand to another. So take the time to measure what kind of liquid volume your device actually holds.

WATER

Since the main component in your cup of coffee is water, you will want it to be as clean and pure as possible.

Quality

Water quality varies state to state and city to city, and older buildings' pipes can also contribute dubious flavors to the mix.

If you're unsure of what's coming out of the tap, a simple solution is an inexpensive pitcher-based water filter, the kind you can buy at most grocery stores. Water filters get rid of unwanted hard minerals and impurities that can damage your brewing equipment and impart unwanted flavors to the coffee.

Always start with cold water. Why? Because you do not want to drink water that comes out of your hot water tank—who knows what lives in that thing! Start with cold water, preferably filtered.

Brew temperature

The ideal water temperature range for brewing coffee is 198-205°F. Water typically reaches its boiling point at 212°F.

Most brewing methods in this book suggest you bring your water to a boil, then leave it off the boil for 30 seconds before starting to brew. This will bring your water into the ideal range. You may notice subtle differences in flavor at the higher and lower temperatures. Feel free to experiment to your taste.

Note: if you live at higher altitudes, your boiling point will be lower, about 203°F, and you may need to scale your brew temperatures accordingly. This means if you live in Denver, by the time the boiling water makes it from the kettle to the coffee pot, it will likely have cooled to an optimum brewing temperature.

★ WATER ★

THE BLOOM

Every brewing method described in this book involves pre-infusing the coffee with slightly less than twice its weight in water and waiting for the grounds to saturate and "bloom" before continuing to pour.

When grounds are saturated in this way, they will puff up in a dome that is quite beautiful to behold. This usually takes between 30 and 60 seconds. Fresher coffee needs to bloom longer.

Coffee holds twice its weight in water before it becomes saturated and begins to drip. So, if you are brewing 24 grams of coffee, you would shoot for pre-infusing with about 48 grams of water. This is why scales make things so much easier. But you can also learn to eyeball it.

Remember that only freshly roasted coffee will truly bloom. Stale coffee will be "flat." You don't want that!

WHICH METHOD?

How much coffee do you need in the morning? Do you want the super-clean cup a paper filter delivers, or do you enjoy the big mouth feel of French press? And how many mouths are you feeding?

Below is a brief summary of the advantages the different methods have to offer:

French press: Presses are available in sizes to meet every need, from serving an individual to a crowd. This method requires little tending, and the pot can be brought to the table and shared. French press coffee has a lot of body as it retains most of the coffee's natural oils and insoluble solids, which make it a chewy, straightforward cup.

Chemex: Still want to serve a crowd—or just yourself—but want a cleaner cup than you get from the French press? Then Chemex is your method. It's a universal tool, elegant and versatile.

Hario: This is a pour-over method with a cone-shaped filter made specifically to brew one cup of coffee at a time. One cup not enough? See the Kalita option.

Kalita: This method, while similar to Hario, allows you to brew a super-sexy little pot of coffee that can be shared with one other person, or is perfect for the two-cup-a-morning coffee drinker.

Cone Filter: You can buy these anywhere, and they come in a variety of sizes; the #4 probably fits the filters for the electric coffee maker you already own. You can even buy a foldable rubber cone, so you can brew your coffee on the road. Generic and reliable.

Electric Coffee Maker: We all have those lazy days when we want to press a button and get in the shower. The key to making coffee maker coffee taste like something you actually want to drink is getting your coffee grind right, and your coffee-to-water ratios correct.

Cold Press: The only method here that takes more than 5 minutes, this is a smooth, cold cup brewed without any heat, yielding a well-rounded, less acidic coffee. Cold brew may be your choice come summer, because it's in your fridge, always ready.

EQUIPMENT

Here are a few items that can help make your life easier and your coffee more delicious:

Burr grinder: A burr grinder is a huge step up from your typical push-top, whirly-bird blade grinder. A burr grinder allows you to adjust the grind in exact increments, yielding coffee ground to an even consistency. Consistent grind equals even extraction.

While your burr grinder may come with a hopper in which you could store your beans, don't. These are usually not airtight and your coffee will go stale. Besides, if you're going to be using a scale, you will be weighing out the amount of coffee you need for each brewing method, eliminating waste.

Scale: When you use a scale, you are able to measure out the exact dose of coffee, and the exact dose of water. This sounds fussy, but the scale actually makes your morning routine dead simple, because with it, you don't even have to eyeball the amounts anymore.

How do you use the scale to save time and brainpower?

Turn on your scale and hit the zero button, also sometimes marked "tare." Tare weight is the weight of the substance being measured minus the weight of the container that holds it—taring is how the cashier at the local salad bar charges you for the weight of your salad but not the weight of the bowl.

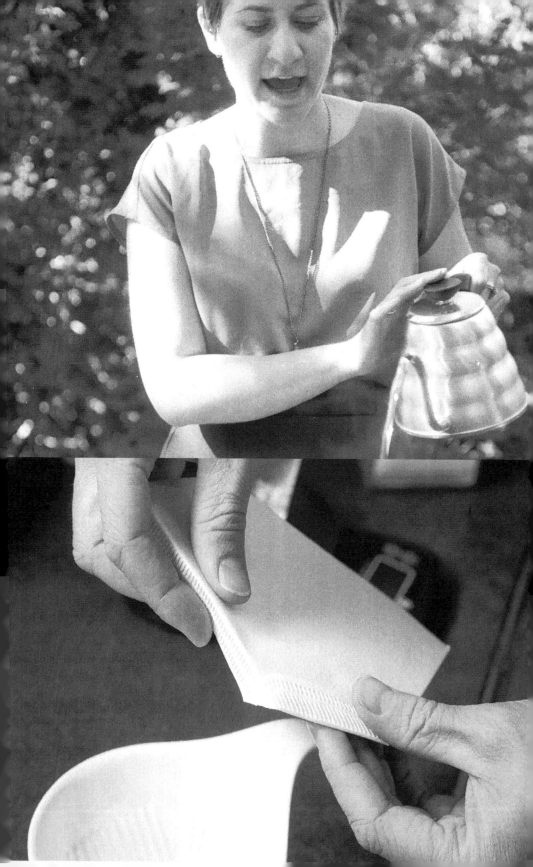

First, weigh out whole bean coffee, then grind it and pour it into a pre-moistened filter. Never pour grounds directly into a dry filter.

Now set your brew vessel and filter on the scale and hit zero/tare again. Now when you start to pour water, the scale will show you the weight of the water you add. If the brew recipe calls for 560 grams of water, you will know exactly when to stop pouring to end up with the perfect coffee-to-water ratio.

Kettle: The key here is to use a gooseneck kettle with a fine-tipped spout that pours from the bottom of the reservoir, such as the Hario Buono Kettle. This design eliminates glugging, and the fine tip gives you control over the stream of water. These kettles can be heated directly on an electric range, but many fans of this kettle heat the water first and use the Hario just to pour—less wear and tear on the kettle this way. Or you can find an electric version, which will save you a step.

Timer: Any timing device will do. You can go out and buy a $10 timer, or use your smartphone or microwave—or maybe you're a 20th century throwback who actually wears a watch. The pour-over methods described in this book provide a target time for when you should be finished pouring your water. The timer will keep you apprised.

That's it, now go make some coffee!

★EQUIPMENT★

4:30

BREW TIME

★

FRENCH PRESS

Grind Level 10

The French press sometimes gets a bad rap in the media, but if you like a coffee that's thick and very rich, with a full mouth feel, it can serve you well. It is one of the easiest coffee-brewing methods, so don't overthink it.

Ristretto Roasters' wholesale manager, Ryan Cross, is known for brewing a perfect French press. "I recommend filtering a French press through a pre-rinsed, pre-heated paper cone," he says, "for a cup that is delicious and clean."

EQUIPMENT LIST

32-ounce French press

65 grams whole bean coffee
(about 2/3 of a cup)

water

DIRECTIONS

Set the kettle to boil.

Preheat the vessel with hot water then pour it out.

Grind the coffee on the coarsest setting and pour it into the glass carafe of the press.

Tap the press gently to level the grounds.

Set your timer for 4:30—but don't start it yet!

When the water boils...

Turn the kettle off and...

Start the timer. Let the water sit off the boil for 30 seconds to bring it down to the perfect temperature for brewing.

Pour water quickly over the ground coffee, filling the carafe halfway.

Wait another 60 seconds. The coffee will bloom in a dome.

When it crests, in 30 to 60 seconds...

Tap the base of the press gently on the counter three times to break up the bloom, then...

Pour water in a gentle circular motion, filling the carafe to an inch below the top.

Set the plunger and press to about one inch below the water line, then lift it up a half-inch.. This action helps avoid French press "lock"and ensures even extraction.

Wait until the timer dings, another 2:30 or so.

Push the plunger all the way down. It should glide so easily you could do it with your pinky.

Pour and drink immediately. If there is brewed coffee remaining in the press, decant it into another vessel to avoid over-extraction.

★FRENCH PRESS★

TROUBLESHOOTING

My plunger is too hard to press down.

"Plunger lock" is a common issue with the French press, and is entirely the result of operator error. Causes include using too fine a grind, failing to allow the coffee time to bloom, failing to "prime" the plunger by depressing it slightly then lifting back up when starting to brew, or a combination of the above.

The coffee isn't hot enough.

If the coffee from your French press gets too cold too quickly, try preheating your carafe by first filling it with hot water, dumping the water, then starting your brewing process. You can also preheat your cups with hot water (halfway up the cup to avoid a hot rim), then dump before pouring in brewed coffee.

The second cup tastes dirty.

The French press is not a "brew and hold" method, as the coffee stays in contact with the grounds for as long as it remains in the carafe. You should be making just as much coffee as you will be pouring and drinking right away. This is the reason no good can come of buying a press with an insulated carafe.

★FRENCH PRESS★

CHEMEX

Grind Level 8

The Chemex is a heat-proof, laboratory grade glass drip coffee maker invented in 1941 by Dr. Peter Schlumbohm. It is part of the permanent collections of the Museum of Modern Art in New York and the Smithsonian.

The Chemex uses a thicker filter paper than the other methods in this book, to support the weight of the saturated coffee. This thicker paper traps more lipids and insoluble solids, yielding coffee that is light, bright and delicately balanced.

EQUIPMENT LIST

Chemex carafe + filter

75 grams whole bean coffee
(about 3/4 of a cup)

900 grams water (32 oz)

DIRECTIONS

Set the kettle to boil.

Nest the filter in the top of the carafe, with the thicker, multi-layered wall of the filter against the pouring spout.

Moisten the filter with enough hot water to wet the entire filter.

Discard any water that drips into the carafe.

Grind the coffee to a coarse level 8 of 10, just finer than for French press.

Shake the carafe gently to level the grounds.

Set your timer for 4:30—but don't start it yet!

When the water boils...

Turn the kettle off and...

Start the timer. Let the water sit off the boil for 30 seconds. This will bring it down to the perfect temperature for brewing.

Dampen the grounds with about 100 grams of water and allow the coffee to bloom, 45 to 60 seconds.

Add more water before the bloom dries.

Pour water in a circular motion, spiraling from the edge to the center and back out again, being careful not to pour directly on the filter. Continue to pour in a circular motion, keeping the coffee/water level just below the rim of the Chemex.

Allow the coffee to drip.

Remove and discard the filter.

Pour and drink immediately.

★ CHEMEX ★

TROUBLESHOOTING

The grounds mount up the sides of the filter.

This means you are pouring too quickly, and probably not
in a neat spiral. Many kettles want to "glug" the water out in
big splashes, making it hard to pour evenly. A gooseneck
kettle will solve this problem, as it has a very small spout that
draws from the bottom of the kettle, letting no air in to cause
those annoying burps and splashes. Remember, pouring too
quickly won't get the caffeine into your veins any sooner, as
the coffee will drip through the filter in its own good time.

The coffee isn't hot enough.

If the coffee from your Chemex gets too cold too quickly,
try preheating your carafe by first filling it with hot water,
dumping the water, then starting your brewing process. You
can also preheat your cups with hot water (halfway up the
cup to avoid a hot rim), then dump before pouring in brewed
coffee.

I taste filter paper.

You might have forgotten to dampen the filter before adding
your grounds, or you might not have poured enough water
through the filter during the pre-rinse. Get it good and wet. If
you still taste paper, consider investing in a metal mesh cone.

KALITA

Grind Level 6

The flat-bottomed Kalita filter is the perfect means of producing coffee for two in the morning—or two cups for one thirsty individual.

The Kalita produces a brighter cup than the French press because it employs a paper filter.

EQUIPMENT LIST

Kalita cone dripper + filter + carafe

33 grams whole bean coffee
(about 1/3 of a cup)

540 grams water (about 19 oz)

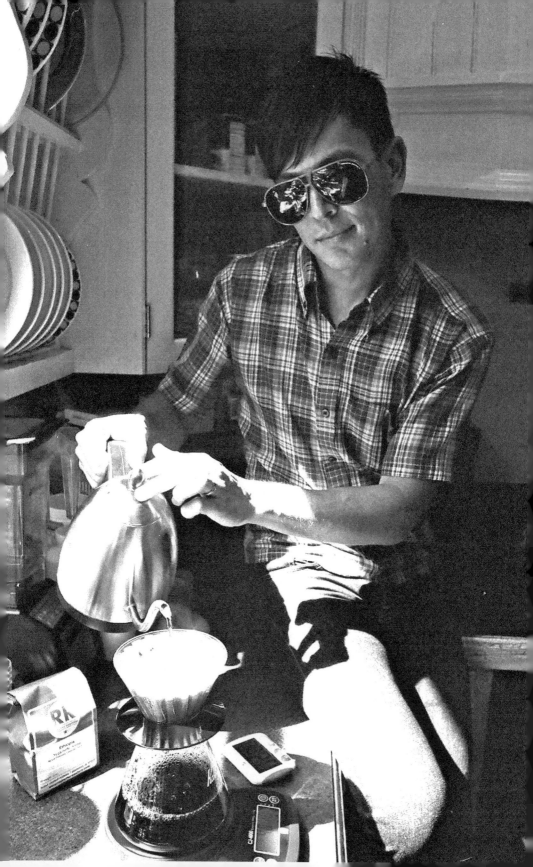

DIRECTIONS

Set the kettle to boil.

Nest the paper filter in the cone.

Dampen the filter with a little hot water. Pour in the center, so you keep the Kalita's signature wave shape intact.

Discard any water that drips into the carafe.

Weigh out your beans.

Grind the coffee to medium-coarse, level 6, and pour it into the paper filter.

Shake the cone dripper gently to level the grounds.

Place the cone dripper on top of the carafe.

Set your timer for 3:30—but don't start it yet!

When the water boils...

Turn the kettle off and...

Start the timer. Let the water sit off the boil for 30 seconds to bring it down to the perfect temperature for brewing.

Pour water in a circular motion, starting from the center and moving gently to the outer edge of the filter and back again, until the filter is nearly full.

Allow the coffee to bloom for 30 seconds.

Pour a second time in the same circular motion, again filling the filter. Pour hard enough that the coffee and the water mix together.

Keep pouring whenever the level drops, but in a single column, trying not to agitate the coffee.

Total pouring time = 2:30 to 3 minutes. The grounds should create a flat bed on the bottom of the filter when it has drained.

Drink immediately.

★ KALITA ★

TROUBLESHOOTING

My coffee is dripping faster/slower than the recommended time.

Coffee brewing too fast? Your grind is too coarse. Try grinding the coffee on a finer setting. Coffee brewing too slowly? Your grind is too fine. Try experimenting with a coarser setting. The rate at which your coffee drips will also depend on its country of origin, and how it was processed.

★KALITA★

3:30
BREW TIME
★

CONE FILTER

Grind Level 5

Cone filters are versatile: they come in many sizes,
some making a pot of coffee, others a single cup.
A good starting point is a ratio of 8.25 grams of coffee
to every 4 ounces of water, upping the ratio to taste.
As for filters, you can use a paper filter or a gold one.
The coffee made with the gold filter will require
a slightly coarser grind. It will have a fuller mouth-feel,
but will be harder to clean up after.

EQUIPMENT LIST

Filter cone + filter + carafe or cup

8.25 grams coffee per...

4 oz water

DIRECTIONS

Set the kettle to boil.

Nest the filter in the top of the filter cone. If using paper, fold the seams so it fits nicely.

Dampen the filter with a little hot water, discarding any excess.

Weigh out your beans.

Grind the coffee to medium coarseness, level 5 of 10, and pour it into the filter cone.

Shake the cone gently to level the grounds.

Place the filter cone on top of the cup or carafe you have chosen as a brew vessel.

Set your timer for 3:30—but don't start it yet!

When the water boils turn the kettle off and...

Start the timer. Let the water sit off the boil for 30 seconds to bring it down to the perfect temperature for brewing.

Pour water in a circular motion, moving gently from the center out and back again, until the filter is nearly full. Never pour directly onto the filter.

Allow the coffee to bloom for 30 seconds.

Pour again in the same circular motion, filling the filter. Pour hard enough that the coffee and the water mix together. (If you are brewing a single cup, omit this second pour.)

Keep pouring whenever the level drops, but in a single column, trying not to agitate the coffee.

Total pouring time = 2:30 to 3 minutes. The grounds should create a flat bed on the bottom of the filter when it has drained.

Drink immediately.

★ CONE FILTER ★

3:30
BREW TIME
★

HARIO V60

Grind Level 5

The Hario V60 pour-over method requires slightly more finesse than the other methods described in this book, but yields fine-tuned results in the bargain.
While the Kalita and Melitta pour-over cones have small holes that only allow water to pass through them at a fixed rate, the Hario cone is open and channeled, so that the rate of flow will depend on how quickly— or slowly—you pour. This method is a barista favorite, and lets you geek out on technique while keeping your investment in equipment down.

EQUIPMENT LIST

Hario kettle + Hario V60 cone + filter

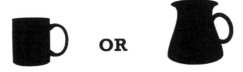

cup or carafe

22 grams coffee (generous 1/4 cup)
340 grams water (about 12 oz)

RR
RISTRETTO ROASTERS

DIRECTIONS

Set the kettle to boil.

Nest the paper filter in the cone, making sure to fold over the side seam so it fits nicely.

Dampen the filter with hot water until you see the Hario's ribs through the filter. Discard any excess water.

Weigh out your beans.

Grind the coffee to medium-fine coarseness, level 5 of 10, and pour it into the filter cone.

Shake the cone gently to level the grounds.

Set the cone on the mug or carafe into which you will brew.

Make a small crater in the coffee with a spoon. Do not compact the coffee.

Set your timer for 3:30—but don't start it yet!

When the water boils turn the kettle off and...

Start the timer. Let the water sit off the boil for 30 seconds to bring it down to the perfect temperature for brewing.

Using a quick, circular motion the size of a quarter, pour 48 grams of water directly in the center of the crater. Allow to bloom for 30 seconds.

When the bloom begins to deflate...

Pour in small circles, breaking the crust of the bloom.

Create a "caldera"—a build-up of coffee along the sides of the cone—to keep the water from flowing directly down the sides of the filter.

Drink immediately.

★HARIO V60★

5:00

BREW TIME
★

ELECTRIC COFFEE MAKER

Grind Level 5

Good morning, Mr. Coffee!
A lot of folks have these, if not at home than at the office,
so while it is not the coffee connoisseur's first choice,
there are ways to make it work for you.

Look for a high-wattage coffee maker. Most drip makers don't
get the water hot enough to properly brew,
so the higher the wattage the better.

Brewing into an insulated carafe is also better for your coffee's
longevity than a glass carafe that sits on a heating element.

EQUIPMENT LIST

Electric coffee maker + filter

65 grams whole bean coffee
(about 2/3 of a cup)

1120 grams water (40 oz)

RR

DIRECTIONS

The ratios given are for a 10 cup Technivorm Thermal Brewer which brews into a 1.25 liter thermal carafe.

Fill the brewer's reservoir with cold water.

Nest the filter in the brewer's basket.

Dampen the filter with a little hot water.

Weigh out your beans.

Grind the coffee to level 5 of 10 and pour it into the filter cone. Note: If you are using a flat-bottomed filter, grind for level 6.

Shake the basket gently to level the grounds and place in the machine.

Turn the brewer on and allow the coffee to drip...

Pour and drink within 30 minutes.

Note: If coffee sits on a heating element longer than 30 minutes, it begins to lose its natural sweetness as the flavor solids dissipate, rendering it bitter, sour, or both. Don't do it.

★ELECTRIC COFFEE MAKER★

COLD BREW

Grind Level 10

Cold brewing produces a smooth, velvety cup. While commercial brewers like the Toddy are available, you can make a fine cold brew with just a French press and a refrigerator—and patience, as this coffee takes a good 12 hours to brew.

You can make either hot or cold coffee breverages with the resulting filtered concentrate, which will last 7 to 10 days in the refrigerator. If you are having a dinner party, making concentrate in advance can be a good way to have enough coffee on hand to serve 8-10 people.

If you are used to adding sugar to your coffee, try the cold brew without—you might be surprised.

EQUIPMENT LIST

French press carafe

100 grams whole bean coffee
(about 1 cup)

900 grams water (32 oz)

DIRECTIONS

Weigh out your beans.

Grind the coffee to level 10 out of 10 and pour it into the carafe.

Add two cups of room-temperature water and allow the coffee to bloom for about ten minutes.

Add the remaining water.

Stir.

Cover with either the French press lid (but do not plunge!) or some plastic wrap.

Refrigerate overnight, or about 12 hours. Or brew at room temperature, which gives the coffee more body.

Plunge coffee and decant into a second receptacle.

If you want a lighter body, decant through a paper filter.

Store in the refrigerator.

Use diluted 1:1 with fresh water for cold coffee drinks.

★ COLD BREW ★

DIN JOHNSON

Din Johnson grew up in Portland, Oregon. A former skate punk, Johnson worked as a bouncer, barkeep and painting contractor up and down the West Coast before returning to Portland to found Ristretto Roasters in 2005 with the help of his wife, Nancy Rommelmann. Since then, Ristretto has grown from boutique cafe with an on-site vintage roaster into a thriving business with an independent roastery and coffee lab, and three architecturally distinctive and popular cafes in urban Portland.

Ristretto's coffees have been recommended to readers of *Travel + Leisure, Sunset Magazine* and *Bon Appetit*, and in 2011, Zagat named Ristretto one of "The 10 Coolest Coffee Shops Across the US."

"My biggest thing is making good coffee approachable," Johnson told the Oregon Business Journal in 2012. This book, written in close collaboration with Ristretto's staff of baristas, many of whom have been with the company since it opened, is a direct outgrowth of that philosophy.

RistrettoRoasters.com

Made in the USA
San Bernardino, CA
28 December 2014